HOW TO FIND YOUR PASSION AND PURPOSE

FOUR EASY STEPS TO DISCOVER A JOB YOU WANT
AND LIVE THE LIFE YOU LOVE

CASSANDRA GAISFORD

This book is dedicated to love.
And to Lorenzo, my Templar Knight,
who encourages and supports me
to make my dreams possible...
And to all my clients
who have shared their passions with me,
and allowed me to help make their dreams come true.
Thank you
for inspiring me.

CONTENTS

HOW TO FIND YOUR PASSION AND PURPOSE: FOUR EASY STEPS TO DISCOVER A JOB YOU WANT AND LIVE THE LIFE YOU LOVE

Cassandra Gaisford, BCA, Dip Psych

PRAISE FOR HOW TO FIND YOUR PASSION AND PURPOSE

"This little book on a BIG topic that resonates with me packs a lot of wisdom that is worth investing time in. Cassandra challenges us to "Dare to Dream!" Take the time and make the effort to find the work you feel passionate about; You could read this in less than two hours and be on your way to sculpting out a new way of living if you're not living your passionate lifestyle yet."

~ Scott.B. Allan, Author of #1 bestseller *Empower Your Thoughts*

"This excellent little book is quick to read but left me with much to think about and many practical steps to take to find my passion and incorporate it into my life. There are several free resources to download which increase the worth of this already very valuable book."

~ Jenny Cliff, Author of *The Music Inside*

"*How to Find Your Passion and Purpose* is a positive and enabling companion and offers much. It encourages us to identify our passion and interests, to live from our core values and use our signature strengths creatively. It highlights that it's never too late to make changes, to get on the path of true fulfillment and make a living. Dig into this book and let Cassandra be your guide, inspiration and coach as she calls forth your creativity and gives practical steps to take you where you need to go next. Step into this ride joyfully and create your future."

~ **Jasbindar Singh, Business Psychologist and Author of** *Get Your Groove Back*

FOREWORD

By Jasbindar Singh

How to Find Your Passion and Purpose is brimming with passion, ideas and inspiration as Cassandra Gaisford walks her talk in living her purpose and showing the way for others wanting to do the same. Given that we spend so much of our lives working, it is vital that we do what we have energy and passion for. We are living and working longer so it is very important that we align what we do with our deeper sense of calling and what gives us meaning and purpose.

I am delighted to say that this book is a wonderful compendium for anyone wishing to design their future as they cull the best of their present and past and shape their new destiny.

How to Find Your Passion and Purpose is a positive and enabling companion and offers much. It encourages us to identify our passion and interests, to live from our core values and use our signature strengths creatively. It highlights that it's never too late to make changes, to get on the path of true fulfilment and make a living.

Dig into this book and let Cassandra be your guide, inspiration and coach as she calls forth your creativity and gives practical steps to take you where you need to go next. Step into this ride joyfully and start creating the future today.

~ Jasbindar Singh, Business Psychologist and Author of *Get Your Groove Back*

AUTHOR'S NOTE

This book is a concise guide to making the most of your life. It began its journey some years ago as *The Passion Pack* – a set of 40 cards created to help people live and work with passion.

The vision was simple: a few short, easy to digest tips for time-challenged people who were looking for inspiration and practical strategies to encourage positive change.

From my own experience, I knew that people didn't need a large wad of words to feel inspired, gain clarity and be stimulated to take action.

In coaching and counselling sessions I'd encourage my clients to ask a question they would like answered. The questions could be specific, such as, 'How can I make a living from my passion?' Or vague, for example, 'What do I most need to know?'

Then I'd ask them to pick a card at random. Without fail, they were astounded by the card's potent relevance. Disbelieving eyes widened in astonishment as they read either the quote or the main message they received. Many would say, "These cards are magic."

Orders flooded in from global recruitment consultancies, primary schools, colleges, universities, not-for-profit organisations, financial institutions and other multi-national commercial entities. I was asked to speak at conferences around the world about the power of passion. It was amazing to see how popular and successful *The Passion Pack* became, transcending age, gender, and socio-economic differences.

In this era of information obesity the need for simple, life-affirming messages is even more important. If you are looking for inspiration and practical tips, in short, sweet sound bites, this guide is for you.

Similarly, if you are a grazer, or someone more methodical, this guide will also work for you. Pick a page at random, or work through the steps sequentially. I encourage you to experiment, be open-minded and try new things. I promise you will achieve outstanding results.

Clive, a 62-year-old man who had suffered work-related burnout, did! He thought that creating a passion journal, *Tip 10* in this guide, was childish – something other stressed executives in his men's support group would balk at. But once he'd taken up the challenge he told me enthusiastically,

"They loved it!" They are using their passion journals to visualize, gain clarity, and create their preferred futures. Clive is using it to help manifest his new purpose-driven coaching business.

Let experience be your guide. Give your brain a well-needed break. Let go of 'why', and embrace how you *feel*, or how you want to feel. Honor the messages from your intuition and follow your path with heart.

Laura, who at one stage seemed rudderless career-wise, did just that. She was guided to *Tip 14: Who Inspires You?* Following that, her motivation to live and work like those she looked up to sparked a determination to start her own business. It was that simple.

At the time of writing I've just turned to Tip *31: Fear Of Success.* It's a timely reminder of just how far following my passion has taken me – the shy girl who was once afraid of being seen. The quote is as apt for me as I feel it may be for you:

"YOUR PLAYING SMALL DOESN'T SERVE THE WORLD."

Here's to living with passion and purpose!

Are you afraid of criticism? In 2019 I released a book called *The Little Princess*. It's based on the true-story of how I was attached and criticised when I shared my dream to create a tool to help people follow their passion and purpose. If you're afraid of standing out you may enjoy reading The Little Princess. Discover how I found my courage, and aligned with my purpose to create a life of joy, passion, prosperity, and fulfilment.

INTRODUCTION

"Mary Oliver says in one of her poems, 'Tell me, what is it that you plan to do with your one wild and precious life?' Me, I intend to live passionately."
Isabel Allende, Novelist

Finding a job you want and living a life you love is impossible without passion, enthusiasm, zest, inspiration and the deep satisfaction that comes from doing something that delivers you some kind of buzz.

Yet, it's staggeringly, and dishearteningly, true that many people don't know what they are passionate about, or how they can turn it into a rewarding career. Some research suggests that only 10% of people are living and working with passion. Hence my passion for passion and helping create more positive change in the world.

If you're like many people who don't know what they are passionate about or what gives your life meaning and purpose, this book will help provide the answers.

If you have been told it's not realistic to work and live with passion, this book will help change your mindset.

Together we'll help you get your mojo back, challenge your current beliefs and increase your sense of possibility. By tapping into a combination of practical career strategies, Law of Attraction principles, and the spiritual powers of manifestation, you'll reawaken dreams, boost your self-awareness, empower your life and challenge what you thought was possible.

We'll do this in an inspired yet structured way by strengthening your creative thinking skills, boosting your self-awareness and helping you identify your non-negotiable ingredients for career success and happiness. Little steps will lead naturally to bigger leaps, giving you the courage and confidence to follow your passion and fly free towards career happiness and life fulfilment.

What you're about to read isn't another self-help book; it's a self-empowerment book. It offers ways to increase your self-knowledge. From that knowledge comes the power to create a life worth living.

How to Find Your Passion and Purpose will help you:

- Explore and clarify your passions, interests, and life purpose
- Build a strong foundation for happiness and success
- Value your gifts, and talents and confirm your work-related strengths
- Direct your energies positively toward your preferred future
- Strengthen your creative thinking skills, and ability to identify possible roles you would enjoy, including self-employment
- Have the courage to follow your dreams and super-charge the confidence needed to make an inspired change
- Find your point of brilliance

Let's look briefly at what each chapter in this book will cover:

Step One, "The Call For Passion" will help you explore the meaning of passion and discover the benefits of following it, and consequences of ignoring your passion. You'll identify any passion blocking beliefs and intensify passion-building beliefs to boost your chances of success.

Step Two, "Discover Your Passion," will help you to identify your own sources of passion and passion criteria. What you'll discover may be a complete surprise and open up a realm of opportunities you've never considered.

Step Three, "Passion at Work," will assist you in identifying career options and exploring ways to develop your career in light of your passions and life purpose.

Step Four, "Live Your Passion," looks at passion beyond the world of work and ways to achieve greater balance and fulfilment. You'll also identify strategies to overcome obstacles and to maximise your success.

How to Find Your Passion and Purpose concludes with showing you how to identify your point of brilliance.

How To Use This Book—Your Virtual Coach

To really benefit from this book think of it as your 'virtual' coach—answer the questions and complete the additional exercises that you'll find in the chapters and free extras.

Questions are great thought provokers. Your answers to these questions will help you gently challenge current assumptions and gain greater clarity about your goals and desires.

All the strategies are designed to facilitate greater insight and to help you integrate new learnings. Resist the urge to just process information in your head. We learn best by doing. Research has repeatedly proven that the act of writing deepens your knowledge and understanding.

For example, a study conducted by Dr. David K. Pugalee, found that journal writing was an effective instructional tool and aided learning. His research found that writing helped people organize and describe internal thoughts and thus improve their problem solving-skills.

Henriette Klauser, Ph.D., also provides compelling evidence in her book, *Write It Down and Make It Happen*, that writing helps you clarify what you want and enables you to make it happen.

Writing down your insights is the area where people like motivational guru Tony Robbins, say that the winners part from the losers, because the losers always find a reason not to write things down. Harsh but perhaps true!

Keeping A Passion Journal

A passion journal is also a great place to store sources of inspiration to support you through the career planning and change process. For some tips to help you create your own inspirational passion journal, go to the media page on my website and watch my television interview and interview with other experts here:

http://www.cassandragaisford.com/media

This Book Is Magical

This book proves less really is more. Sometimes all it takes to radically transform your life is one word, one sentence, one powerful but simple strategy to ignite inspiration and reawaken a sense of possibility.

I have successfully used the knowledge I'm sharing with you in this book professionally with my clients and personally during numerous reinventions.

I stand by every one of the 4 steps and the 40+ strategies you will learn here, not just because they are grounded in strong evidence-based, scientific and spiritual principles, but also because I have successfully used them to create turnaround, after turnaround in nearly every area of my life.

How to Find Your Passion and Purpose is the culmination of all that I have experienced and all that I have learned, applied and taught others for over two decades. I don't practice what I preach; I preach what I have practiced—because it gets results.

Why Did I Write This Book?

If you are curious about *The Passion Pack* and why I created *How To Find Your Passion and Purpose*, you may like to check out my blog post here:

http://www.cassandragaisford.com/2557-2/

Setting You Up For Success

"Aren't you setting people up for failure?" a disillusioned career coach once challenged me.

Twenty-five years of cumulative professional experience as a career coach and counsellor, helping people work with passion and still pay the bills, answers that question. I'm setting people up for success. I'm not saying it will happen instantly, but if you follow the advice in this book, it will happen. I promise.

I've proven repeatedly, both personally and professionally, that thinking differently and creatively, rationally and practically, while also harnessing the power of your heart, and applying the principles of manifestation, really works. In this book, I'll show you why —and how.

A large part of my philosophy and the reason behind my success with clients is my fervent belief that to achieve anything worthy of life you need to follow your passion. And I'm in good company.

As media giant Oprah Winfrey once said, "Passion is energy. Feel the power that comes from focusing on what excites you."

Passion's Pay Cheque

By discovering your passion and purpose you will tap into a huge source of potential energy and prosperity. Pursuing your passion can be profitable on many levels:

- When you do what you love, your true talent will reveal itself; passion can't be faked
- You'll be more enthusiastic about your pursuits
- You'll have more energy to overcome obstacles
- You will be more determined to make things happen
- You will enjoy your work
- Your work will become a vehicle for self-expression
- Passion will give you a competitive edge
- You'll enjoy your life and magnetize positive experiences toward you

Without passion, you don't have energy, and without energy you have nothing.

You have to let love, desire, and passion, not fear or ambivalence or apathy, propel you forward. Yet worryingly, research suggests that less than 10% of people are following their passion. Perhaps that's why there is so much unhappiness in the world.

Don't waste another day feeling uninspired. Don't be the person who spends a life of regret, or waits until they retire before they follow their passions, be you. Don't be the person too afraid to make a change for the better, or who wishes they could lead a significant life. Make the change now. Before it's too late.

EXTRA SUPPORT: COMPANION WORKBOOK

How to Find Your Passion and Purpose (the book) offers you information about overcoming adversity, building resilience and finding joy. Reading a book is great but applying the teachings and writing things down in a dedicated space helps bring the learning alive, deepens your self awareness, and enables you to make real world change. Reading gives you knowledge, but reflecting upon and applying that knowledge creates true empowerment.

By writing and recording your responses you're rewriting the story of your life. As Seth Godin states, "Here's the thing: The book that will most change your life is the book you write. The act of writing things down, of justifying your actions, of being cogent and clear, and forthright—that's how you change."

The *How to Find Your Passion and Purpose Companion Workbook* will support you through the learning and show you how to create real and meaningful change in your life...simply and joyfully.

Reach For Your Dreams

Passion, happiness, joy, fulfilment, love—call it what you will, my deepest desire is that this book encourages you to reach for your dreams, to never settle, to believe in the highest aspirations you have for yourself.

You have so many gifts, so many talents that the world so desperately needs. We need people like you who care about what they do, who want to live and work with passion and purpose.

I promise that if you follow the steps in this book you'll discover what you really want to do, clarify what you can do, and create powerful but simple strategies to make your dream a reality. You'll find a job that you love, one that adds more joy to your life and gives you a sense of meaning, purpose, and fulfilment.

And what I can promise you is this—whatever your circumstances, it's never too late to re-create yourself and your life. So, what are you waiting for?

Let's get started!

STEP 1: THE CALL FOR PASSION

Read through the following tips numbered 1-8 and consider your responses to each strategy. You may want to keep notes about your responses in a special book or journal.

Tips 1-4 ask you to consider what you believe passion is and to identify what passion means to you. What role do you think passion should have in your life? Do you have any passion-blocking beliefs? What are your passion-building beliefs?

Tips 5-8 cover the consequences of ignoring your passion. How do you think not pursuing your dreams might affect you? How has it affected other people you know? What are your goals, hopes, and dreams for your future? What will having more passion in your life do for you?

WHAT IS PASSION?

**"Nothing great in the world
has been accomplished without passion."**
G.W.F.Hegel, Philosopher

To be passionate is to be fully alive. Being passionate is a vital part of being human.

Passion is about emotion, feeling, zest and enthusiasm.

Passion is about intensity, fervour, ardor, and zeal.

Passion is about fire.

Passion is about eagerness and preoccupation.

Passion is about excitement and animation.

Passion is about determination and self-belief.

PASSION FOR ALL

**"One person with passion is better
than 40 people merely interested."**
EM Forster, Writer

Every human being is capable of passion. But many people think they
are not.

Remember, different people are passionate in different ways.
Many people think that being passionate only means being loud or
extroverted.

This isn't true at all. Many passionate people are shy or quiet or
reserved. Passionate people come in all shapes, sizes, and ages. You
can pursue your passion at any age and stage of your life.

WHAT IS TRUE FOR YOU?

WHAT CAN PASSION DO?

**"Without passion, man is a mere latent force
and possibility, like the flint which awaits the shock
of the iron before it can give forth its spark."**
Henri-Frederic Amiel, Writer

Passion helps people lead bigger lives.
Passion is an indispensable part of success.
Passion helps people achieve.
Passion energises people.
Passion liberates people. It lets them be themselves.
Passion opens up fresh horizons.
Passion is good for your health and helps you live longer.

What will passion do for you?

REALITY CHECK ON PASSION

**"A human being is not one in pursuit of happiness
but rather in search of a reason to be happy."**
Viktor Frankl, Psychologist

Passion is not always fun. Like anything worthwhile, pursuing your passion often involves great commitment, hard work, and sacrifice.

Passionate people are prepared to give up things to live a more passionate life. Passionate people are prepared to take risks and cope with failure.

The compensation is a bigger, fuller, more interesting life with drive and purpose.

WHAT ARE you prepared to trade-off to be more passionate? What are you prepared to change in your life? What would stop you?

YOUR BODY BAROMETER

"I've got a great ambition to die
of exhaustion rather than boredom."
Angus Grossart, Writer

When you don't do the things you love your health can suffer. Common signs of neglecting your passion can include, headaches, insomnia, tiredness, depression, and irritability.

The body never lies, however, many people soldier on ignoring the obvious warning signs their body is giving them. It's easy to rationalise these feelings away, but the reality is your body is screaming out for something different. Have the courage to say 'enough' and pursue a more satisfying alternative.

WHEN YOU FEEL unfulfilled what do you notice? How does this differ from times when you are passionate?

REGRET

**"The worst thing one can do is be aware
of what one wants and not pursue it,
to spend years regretting things
never achieved or experiences never had."**
Jim Rohn, Writer

Some people, who in their hearts know that they are capable of much more, never pursue their heart's desire. Regret because of a life not fully lived is a major source of depression, stress, and anger for many people.

You only get one shot at life. Don't spend it regretting opportunities you never took and dreams you never lived.

WHAT WOULD you do if you were 10 times bolder?

THE COMFORT RUT

**"Verily the lust for comfort murders the passion of the soul,
and then walks grinning to the funeral."**
Kahil Gibran, Writer

Many people trade off their deeper passions for material comforts
and status that can only ever give fleeting satisfaction. They get stuck
in the comfort rut. Outwardly, they appear successful but in fact, they
are deeply unfulfilled.

We all like to be comfortable, to do well and be well off, but the
comfort rut is a bit like wearing an old shoe – you just keep putting it
on because it feels familiar. But in your heart of hearts you know
you've outgrown it and it's time to change.

BEING true to your self can be the most comfortable feeling of all.
How will living more authentically feel to you?

THE POWER OF PASSION

"Passion is the fire that drives us to express
who we really are. Never deny passion,
for that is to deny who you are
and who you truly want to be."
Neale Walsch, Author

When people are pursuing something they are passionate about their energy, drive and determination is infinite. They become like pieces of elastic able to stretch to anything and accommodate any setback.

People immobilised by fear and passivity snap like a twig. They lack resilience.

Passion gives people a reason for living and the confidence, and drive to pursue their dreams.

RECORD all the reasons why you want more passion in your life. What are all the benefits that will flow?

** FREE BONUS **

Download the free *Passion Journal Workbook* here>>https://dl.
bookfunnel.com/aepj97k2n1

I hope you enjoy it—it's dedicated to helping you live and work with
passion, resilience and joy.

You'll also be subscribed to my newsletter and receive free giveaways,
new release advance alerts and inspirational tips to help you live and
work with passion, joy, and prosperity. Opt out at anytime.

STEP 2: DISCOVER YOUR PASSION

The tips numbered 9-16 will help you to identify your own sources of passion and passion criteria. Answer the questions found on each page and complete the exercises suggested.

Try to be open-minded and consider all possible sources of passion. Be patient and maintain faith. Identifying your passion may not happen overnight, but it will happen if you allow yourself to dream a little and to notice the times you feel more passionate.

Your sources of passion may be a complete surprise. It may be something you have not even considered before. Judge not what you feel passionate about – see only if it serves you and who you want to be.

When are the times you feel most energetic and fully alive? Who were you with? What were you doing? Did time seem to fly?

PASSION'S CLUES

**"Passion is a lot like 'love'. It is difficult,
probably impossible, to define in precise terms,
but easy to see and feel when it is present."**
Charles Kovess, Writer

How will you know if you are passionate? Some common signs include:

- A burning desire or hunger
- A feeling of inspiration
- A feeling in the pit of the stomach
- A sense of excitement
- A state of arousal
- A feeling of limitless energy
- A clarity of vision
- A feeling that nothing is too much trouble
- A sense of caring deeply
- A feeling of contentment

KEEP A PASSION JOURNAL

**"Happiness is a butterfly, which when pursued,
is always beyond your grasp, but which,
if you will sit down quietly may alight upon you."**
Nathaniel Hawthorne, Writer

This is where finding your passion and manifesting your preferred future really happens. I've been keeping a passion journal for years and so many things I've visualized and affirmed on the pages, are now my living realities.

Keep track of the times you notice clues to your passion. Record these moments in an inspirational journal so that they don't get lost or forgotten.

Adding quotes, articles, pictures, and insights from this book – anything that reinforces feelings of passion – will really make your journal come alive.

Gain greater awareness of what drives your passion by asking yourself, "Why am I passionate about this?"

Look for the themes and patterns that build up over time. Keep your passion alive by referring to it regularly and looking for more ways to add passion to your life.

IF YOU NEED MORE HELP to find and live your life purpose you may prefer to take my online course, and watch inspirational and practical videos and other strategies to help you to fulfil your potential.

Follow your passion and purpose to prosperity—online coaching program

Easily discover your passion and purpose, overcoming barriers to success, and create a job or business you love with my self-paced online course.

Gain unlimited lifetime access to this course, for as long as you like—across any and all devices you own. Be supported by me and gain practical, inspirational, easy-to-access strategies to achieve your dreams.

To start achieving outstanding personal and professional results with absolute certainty and excitement. **Click here to enrol or find out more—the-coaching-lab.teachable.com/p/follow-your-passion-and-purpose-to-prosperity**

SOURCES OF PASSION

"Judge not about which you feel passionate. Simply notice it, then see if it serves you, given who and what you wish to be."
Neale Walsch, Writer

Passion goes in all directions. It can be as tangible as a job or car or a house or as intangible as a dream or an idea. You could be passionate about anything:

- A cause
- Analysing things
- Books
- Sports
- Clothes
- Computers
- The future
- A belief
- A movie star
- An idea

- Astrology
- Saving the planet
- Your family

Or something else.

WHAT CAPTURES your interest and attention? List as many things as you can that you could be, or are, passionate about.

FOCUS ON YOUR STRENGTHS

"Where talent and interest intersect
expect a masterpiece."
John Ruskin, Painter

We often take our 'natural knacks' or gifts for granted. However, the skills that are easiest for us can provide a good clue to areas we are most passionate about. Sometimes others have a greater awareness of our strengths and areas of passion than we do!

What skills and talents come most naturally to you?
What strengths do others notice and admire?
What are the other skills and strengths that give you a buzz?

WRITE these insights in your passion journal. Add to it and review it regularly.

. . .

PASSION FLOWS, it can't be forced. Don't underestimate the things that come easiest for you.

WHAT PRESSES YOUR BUTTONS

"The world often continues to allow evil
because it isn't angry enough."
Bede Jarrett, Writer

Passionate anger, constructively used, could become the fuel that drives you, the fuel that drives your passion.

WHAT PRESSES YOUR BUTTONS? It may be specific things going on in your life now or wider issues about life in general, such as injustice, racism etc. Gain greater awareness by exploring why your buttons are being pushed.

ARE there any ways you could you use your anger to benefit others and bring about positive change?

WHO INSPIRES YOU?

**"Inspiring people are like vitamins
for our souls."**
Sark, Writer

Who or what inspires you? Think about the sorts of books and magazines you love to read, or people and things you love to be around. What about them is interesting to you?

LOOK for your heroes and allow others' enthusiasm and passion to excite you! Play detective. Do some research, go and talk to people who are passionate about some aspect of their life, read books about inspiring people or themes that really capture your imagination.

WHAT COULD you do to get more inspired?

A SENSE OF CARING DEEPLY

"To succeed you have to believe in something with such a passion that it becomes a reality."
Anita Roddick, Businesswoman

Real passion is more than a fad or fleeting enthusiasm. It can't be turned on and off like a tap. It's a full-bodied belief or commitment to something.

WHAT DO you care deeply about? Discovering all the things that you feel strongly about is not always easy. Look for some clues to your beliefs by catching the times you use words such as "should" or "must."

What do you really believe in? It might be honesty, openness, freedom, equality, or justice. Record your insights in your passion journal.

WHAT ARE YOUR VALUES?

"What we seek with passionate longing, here and there, outside and beyond; we find at last within ourselves."
Cassandra Gaisford, Author

Your values are your deep, personal needs, and the things that are truly important to you. They represent who you are, who you want to be and what you want to contribute to the world.

You may have a deep need to be creative, to help others, to entertain people or to change the world. Anything.

When your values are met there can be an incredible sense of joy, but value conflicts can also be a powerful clue to your passions.

Identify and acknowledge your values.
What do you really need to feel satisfied?

STEP 3: PASSION AT WORK

Tips 17-26 in this section will help you to identify and explore work options and ways to develop your career in light of your passions.

Tips 18-19 ask you to consider what your beliefs are about the role of passion in the workplace. Is finding a job you love a realistic expectation? What role do you think passion should play in your work life?

Exercises in this section will also help you isolate your passion criteria for job satisfaction. What do need, and what do you wish to contribute, to feel passionate about your work?

Tips 20-26 will help you generate lots of possible career alternatives and to decide on your best-fit career options. Ask yourself why you consider these your best choices. Do they meet your passion criteria? What are some of the steps you need to take in order to make these options a reality?

JOB SATISFACTION

**"When you do something you love
you'll never work again."**
Confucius, Philosopher

We spend too much time at work to give up on passion, but some
people think that you save the things you like for a hobby or for when
you retire.

The truth is you are unlikely to find real satisfaction or meaning in
your work unless it engages you as a person and delivers some kind of
buzz.

Passionate employees are good for business too. People who love
their work are productive, happy and inspired.

What role should passion play in your working life?

YOUR BUZZ FACTORS

**"There is no mistaking love. You feel it in your heart.
It is the common fibre of life."**
Elizabeth Kubler-Ross, Psychologist

If you want to feel happy in your job you need to be clear about all the things that make you feel passionate and alive.

Using what you've learned from the previous pages, make a check-list of your buzz factors for job satisfaction. Some things to consider include:

- Your values, beliefs, and interests
- Your strengths and what you love doing
- The sort of work environment that suits you best
- The people you want to work with
- Your personality and what makes you tick

ADD to this checklist any other factors that sustain your passion. Refer to it when making any career decisions.

DARE TO DREAM

**"If we did all the things we are capable of,
we would literally astound ourselves."**
Thomas Edison, Inventor

A great way to generate career options is to let your imagination go wild. To get closer to your true desires try the following exercise:

Imagine you have just been cloned. You are now five people! Each one of you is going to head in a different direction. There are no constraints—money is not an issue and everywhere you want to go they would hire you.

You can get any job you want and you're going to get all the experience you want. What would each person be willing to try? Be bold. Be creative. Be yourself.

Look for the themes.
How could you turn your dream into a reality?
What are all the possible options?

JOB SCULPTING

"Let others lead small lives, but not you. Let others leave their
future in someone else's hands, but not you."
Jim Rohn, Motivational Counsellor

If you are already employed, but not really enjoying it, try the following exercise. It's about identifying your needs and then taking steps to have them met.

Analyse your current job description/job function and isolate the areas you enjoy most and enjoy least.

Now start sculpting by identifying ways you could chip away at the tasks that don't fulfil you and actively adding on the tasks and responsibilities that you are passionate about.

Develop a strategy to make the changes you desire a reality.

By sculpting your dream role, you stop being just a passive reactor and start being a co-creator in your life.

THINK LATERALLY

**"The man who has no imagination
has no wings."**
Muhammad Ali, Boxer

Brainstorm and list as many possible career options as you can that would allow you to fulfill your passion. Think laterally and don't close down too many ideas.

The aim is not to choose but to build an exhaustive list. Make it fun. If you run out of ideas ask friends, family, and others to contribute ideas. Check out websites such as www.careers.govt.nz for job ideas.

Are there any ways to earn an income from your passion that you haven't thought of or that doesn't exist yet?

What economic, social, and cultural changes could lead to a future opportunity for you?

How could you fulfill a need?

ANALYZE YOUR OPTIONS

**"We cannot solve our problems with the same thinking
we used when we created them."**
Albert Einstein, Scientist

Once you have generated a reasonable list, decide on your best options. Start analysing which ones are most achievable for you. How well do they meet your passion criteria and life goals?

Avoid dismissing your ideas prematurely or acting impulsively. It's a good idea to use a variety of thinking styles to assess their suitability and fit. For example ask questions such as:

- What are the facts?
- How do I feel?
- What works? (i.e. strengths and positives)
- What's possible?
- What could go wrong?
- What's the next step I need to take?

REALITY TEST

**"Treat your facts with imagination
but don't imagine your facts."**
Anon

Don't buy into the myth that being passionate about your work is a dream obtainable by only a few. Reality test your own beliefs or fears.

Look for examples of people who are earning an income from pursuing their passion.

Interview for information and inspiration by talking to people already working in areas they are passionate about, or those who are doing the job you want.

Who could you talk to?

What "facts" do you need to check out?

How could you test your reality further?

NETWORK TO SUCCESS

"If you don't ask, you don't get!"
Mahatma Gandhi, Political Leader

Don't be afraid or too proud to ask for help. 80% of all jobs are never advertised and lots of opportunities go unnoticed. Don't let someone else steal your thunder or pip you to the post.

Keeping an ear to the ground and using personal contacts is the key to success. It's not just what you know, but the people you know or could get to know!

Ask your way to success by identifying and proactively networking with everyone who can help you achieve your goal. You don't have to go it alone. Even Sir Edmund Hilary didn't climb Mount Everest by himself!

THE NEW WORLD OF WORK

"If one advances confidently in the direction of his own dreams, and endeavors to live the life which he has imagined he will meet with a success unexpected in common hours."
Henry Thoreau, Philosopher

Remember work doesn't have to be a 9 to 5 drudge.

Change your relationship to work. If you can't do the thing you love full-time you may be able to do it part-time.

Many people today work on a project basis or do several, different jobs instead of having just one career. Others combine salaried work with self-employment on the side.

Working more flexibly like this could help you to get more passion into your life. How could you repackage your working week?

26

GET CAREER-FIT

"Whatever you can do, or dream you can, begin it. Boldness has genius, power, and magic in it."
Goethe, Philosopher

Make sure you are prepared for the new, passionate you! Update your resume ensuring it's tailored to match the opportunities you're pursuing. Brush up on your interview techniques.

Many people feel uncomfortable promoting themselves. If this is you identify strategies that will help you through the self-marketing phase. Remember that you serve nobody by keeping your light under a bushel.

STEP 4: LIVE YOUR PASSION!

Tips numbered 27-40 in this section look at ways to help you inject more passion and purpose into your life.

Tips 27-28 look at passion beyond the world of work and the issue of achieving work/life balance.

Tips 29-33 look at some possible passion barriers. You'll be encouraged to consider any psychological issues that may need to be worked on so that you can fulfil your potential.

Where are you now and what do you want? What could stop you from doing the things you are passionate about? How could you live a more passionate life?

Tips 34-40 suggest strategies to maximise your success and overcome obstacles. How can you take greater responsibility for living a more passionate life? What will you need to do? What will you need to change?

LIVE WITH PASSION

**"People are just as happy
as they make up their minds to be."**
Abraham Lincoln, Political Leader

Doing work that is your passion is the ideal. However, if it isn't possible at this time then try to find other outlets for your passion. Try to add something to your life that you are passionate about. It could be a hobby, sport or volunteer work.

WHAT GROUPS or organisations could you join to experience more of the things you are passionate about?

Are there any opportunities in your community or among your friends?

28

DAILY TONIC

**"Filling your own needs is not something
that you do randomly, it's something that needs
to be done on a regular basis."**
Cassandra Gaisford, Author

Make passion a regular event. Do you regularly spend time doing things you enjoy? Can you do something every day to help keep your passion alive?

Only 15 or 30 minutes a day devoted to activities you love, and to those that move you closer to your dreams, can make a big difference to your health and happiness.

If finding the time or lacking energy is preventing you from doing more of the things you are passionate about, develop a strategy to restore the balance.

LIVING IN THE PASSION ZONE

**"If you allow your fears to keep you from flying
you will never reach your height."**
India Arie, Singer

Why don't more people pursue their passions?

We have to try and live and work in the passion zone as much as possible. It sounds simple, but most people don't. Reasons vary and are numerous, some common ones include:

- Being caught in the comfort-rut
- Fear
- Lack of confidence and self-belief
- Procrastination

WHAT, if anything, is stopping you from pursuing your passion?

Really analyse what holds you back and develop a strategy to over-come any obstacles that may stand in the way of you and your passion.

FEAR OF FAILURE

**"I'd rather be a failure at something I love
than a success at something I hate."**
George Burns, Comedian

In our Western culture, we often spend more time thinking of ways we could fail rather than ways we could succeed.

People also don't give themselves permission to make mistakes or to learn.

When was the last time you tested your fears?

If you felt the fear and did it anyway what's the worst that could happen?

LOOK for and collect examples of people who have turned "failure" into success.

FEAR OF SUCCESS

"It is our light, not our darkness, that most frightens us. We ask ourselves, who am I to be brilliant, successful, talented and fabulous? Actually, who are you NOT to be? Your playing small doesn't serve the world."
Marianne Williamson, Author

Some people don't pursue their potential because they're afraid of success. Success can bring unwanted attention, criticism and the risk of failing.

Success can also be threatening to others who haven't achieved their potential – even your best friends can become your worst critics.

ARE you afraid of standing out? Are you prepared to be a tall poppy even though others may seek to cut you down? How could your success inspire others?

FEAR OF CHANGE

**"Unless we try to do something beyond what we have already
mastered we cannot grow."**
Ronald Osborn, Writer

People often put more energy into resisting change and preserving
the status quo than they do in embracing change.

Changing can be hard work. It means taking a risk and stepping
into the unknown. Some people fear change because they believe they
may lose what they have—even though what they have may be
nothing at all.

For many people change means taking responsibility and ending
years of blaming others, being a victim, or living in denial or in a state
of apathy.

HOW CAN you be empowered and confront your fears safely?

FEAR OF DISAPPOINTMENT

"You can't possibly net the prize if you're thinking about all the possible ways you can miss."
Cassandra Gaisford, Author

Some people die with their music still inside. They opt to cling to the hope of their aspirations rather than the reality of a possible disappointment and the risk of a shattered dream.

What's worse—the disappointment of a few setbacks, or the disappointment of a life spent unfulfilled and filled with regret?

ALL LIFE ARISES out of choice. What choices are you making now?

ALLOW NO DOUBT

"Winners are too busy to be sad, too positive to be doubtful, too optimistic to be fearful, too focused on success."
Cassandra Gaisford, Author

Attitude is everything. Be a guard for your words, thoughts, and feelings. Don't let self-doubt be the thing that pops your balloon.

Be your biggest fan. Back yourself 100%. We all have doubts, but it's amazing how your doubts will disappear once you are doing the things you love.

ARE you your biggest fan or worst enemy? How can you stay positive, confident and optimistic?

GET OVER THE GUILT

**"I cannot give you the formula for success,
but I can give you the formula for failure,
which is, try to please everybody all the time."**
Herbert Bayard Swope, Writer

Many people don't discuss or live their passion because they feel guilty for wanting more from their lives.

They may have low or narrow expectations of what they should be getting out of life. Or they may feel an overwhelming sense of duty to others and they put everything and everyone else first.

They often rationalise their situation with statements like: "Why am I so special? What's wrong with just getting a job and providing for my family?

ARE YOU FEELING GUILTY?

Imagine how being more passionate could change your life and benefit others.

VISUALIZE YOUR PREFERRED FUTURE

**"I do not know how to distinguish
between our waking life and a dream.
Are we not always living the life that we imagine?"**
Henry Thoreau, Philosopher

Visualisation is a powerful technique used by many successful business and sports people. See your way to success.

Try to visualise your preferred future by closing your eyes and imagining a time in the future 1, 5, or 10 years from now. What are you doing? Who is there? How are you feeling? Walk toward the future and look back to today. What steps did you take to get there?

IF YOU SPEND time imagining the future you want, you have without even knowing it begun to make it happen.

MAKE A PASSION ACTION PLAN

**"To accomplish great things,
we must not only act but also dream;
not only believe but also plan."**
Antole France, Writer

Some people think that fate will take care of their future. But the winners in life know that failing to plan is planning to fail.

Written goals, with action points and time frames, are essential if you really want to achieve a more passionate life.

MAKE A PASSION ACTION PLAN. Do something every day to help move you closer to your goal of leading a more passionate life.

Don't forget to tick off and celebrate your achievements along the way to reinforce feelings of success.

SEND YOUR CRITICS AWAY

"Keep away from people who try to belittle your ambitions. Small people always do that, but the really great make you feel that you, too, can become great."
Mark Twain, Writer

If you are steering towards having more passion in your life, people may be jealous or threatened and criticise you. Be passionate anyway!

Don't be put off by negative feedback. Don't wait for others to give approval to your life. Send your critics on a holiday.

Be brave. Be bold. Be firm. Be audacious. You'll soon conquer your fears and convince others.

WHO COULD you look to for inspiration, encouragement, and support? Check out my 2019 release The Little Princess to learn how I sent my critics away!

PERSISTENCE

"Obstacles don't have to stop you. If you run into a wall, don't turn around and give up. Figure out how to climb it, go through it, or work around it."
Michael Jordan, Basketball Legend

Things worth having in life don't always come easily. You have to want something with such a passion that you're willing to persevere in the face of setbacks.

Every time you persist in the face of obstacles your belief in yourself will sky rocket until it reaches the point where you become unstoppable!

HOW PERSISTENT ARE YOU? Do you give up easily? How can you keep yourself motivated to put in the time and energy it may take to move ahead and reach your goals?

WELCOME TO THE PASSION ZONE!

**"If you follow your bliss, doors will open
for you that wouldn't have opened
for anyone else."**
Joseph Campbell, Writer

You've made it! By reading and applying the practical strategies in this book you've taken the first step to leading a happier and more fulfilled life.

Well done! But remember, you're not there yet. Being passionate is an ongoing commitment that takes time and effort. But just imagine how great you'll feel when you're living your passion.

Keep this book handy and refer to it regularly. It will help you achieve your goals and keep your passion alive. Enlist the support of a career or life coach if you need more help or motivation to reach your goals.

You've completed a tremendous journey. Thank you for allowing me to travel with you.

Before we part company you may find it helpful to summarise all that you have learned by clarifying your passion point or point of brilliance.

YOUR POINT OF BRILLIANCE

Your point of brilliance is where you truly shine. It's your point of passion. It's the intersection of your favorite gifts, and talents, your deepest interests and enthusiasms, and all that motivates, inspires and drives you.

It's the place of fire and alchemy, magnetizing and attracting people, situations and opportunities to you.

But you must show up. You must commit to being authentically you. And you must stand in your own truth. You know what makes you bloom and what makes you wither. You know when you're opening and when you're closing.

Be deliberate and focused in the pursuit of your happiness. Target your intentions on your dreams and desires, and ensure your choices align with what makes you happy.

Get real about your motives. Why do you want to reach your goals? Are your following your path with heart, your life purpose, your true destiny? If you follow your chosen path, will you reach your place of true bliss and authentic happiness?

Are you grounded in your truth, or are you chasing someone else's goals, or the lure of fantasy and ego?

Remember the perfect career and life for you is one that:

- You're passionate about
- Interests you
- Fills you with purpose
- Aligns with your highest values
- Utilises your favourite talents
- Allows you to express yourself
- Fulfils your potential
- Facilitates your growth
- Feeds your mind, body and soul
- Boosts self-esteem and confidence
- Makes you happy
- Fuels your energy
- Gives life
- Enables your goals
- Is your point of brilliance

These are not unrealistic expectations. Target your intentions, and shoot straight for the stars. Don't settle for anything less.

You may find it helpful to summarise the insights you've gained from reading this book. The following exercise can also help you stay on track.

Your Passion Point is your Point of Brilliance

I've always loved John Ruskin's quote, "Where talent, interest and motivation intersect expect a masterpiece."

Using this as your guide, you may like to draw three circles. List your areas of motivation in one (passion, purpose, values, goals etc.); Your interests and obsessions in another; Your favourite skills and talents in the third.

Note where they overlap. This is your internal world, and what I call your Passion Point, or Point of Brilliance.

Surround these three circles with a fourth to enclose them. They symbolise the external world—both the practical earth and the higher heavens.

How Can Your Point Of Brilliance Serve?

To generate more career options, knowing what will be needed or in demand, now and in the future, can yield gold. What needs can you fulfil when you're aligned with your Passion Point? What economic, demographic, social, environmental or other needs can you serve? This is the work you are called to do and where you will truly shine.

It doesn't need to have a massive job title, or be about saving the world. But whatever you chose to do has to fulfil a need. Economics 101—no need, no demand. Of course, if money is no barrier, you are freer to pursue your own needs without this added focus. By doing this you may just create a demand, or make the world a happier place. Importantly, you'll be happy.

Balance The Law of Intention with The Law of Detachment

Remember to balance the Law of Intention with The Law of Detachment. Nothing you want is upstream. Resist the urge to panic, if things don't happen as quickly as you'd like. Go with the flow.

Trust. Cultivate faith. Believe. Allow no doubt.

You may think the outcome has to happen in a certain way, on a certain day, to reach your goal. But human willpower cannot make everything happen. Spirit has its own idea, of how the arrow flies, and upon what wind it travels.

It may not happen overnight, but if you maintain your focus, and take inspired action, and follow your heart, your time will come.

I promise!

If, because of some strange twist of fate it doesn't? At least you tried. A life of no regrets - now that's worth striving for.

"Listen to your gut but sometimes do it anyway. Playing safe is easy but boring."

Katie Couric, Yahoo Global News Anchor and Cancer Awareness Campaigner

AFTERWORD

You've heard the call, you know what brings you joy, contentment and bliss. You've found your capabilities, your aspirations, your longings, and your hidden talents. You've found your passion and you know what makes you happy.

You now have all you need to embark on new experiences and to make life-affirming choices. You have all the seeds to plant new beginnings. You may feel a knot in your gut as you prepare to make a leap, but you're excited.

Your possibilities are infinite. You are empowered and in complete control of your life. Have a foot in the future but stay grounded in the present. Have faith and trust in yourself and your abilities. Plant the seeds of your aspirations, nurture and protect them, and watch them grow into the prosperous fruits of your passion.

Take a leap of faith and venture forth. Work and live with passion!

In gratitude and with love,

Cassandra

p.s. **I'm super excited about my release of *The Little Princess*.**

It's a timeless charm which tells the story of a young woman who leaves the safety of fitting in with everyone else, to follow her heart. Be inspired by this journey to transformation and self-acceptance, and self-belief as she learns to overcome the vagaries of adult behaviour. Her personal odyssey culminates in a voyage of self-belief, passion, and purpose.

Guess what?! It's autobiographical and tells the story of how I was criticised and shamed when I first shared my idea for The Passion Pack. Importantly, it shares what I did to overcome obstacles, heed the call for courage and dare to lead.

Available now from all excellent online bookstores in audio, eBook and paperback.

FOLLOW YOUR PASSION TO PROSPERITY ONLINE COURSE

If you need more help to find and live your life purpose you may prefer to take my online course, and watch inspirational and practical videos and other strategies to help you to fulfil your potential.

Follow your passion and purpose to prosperity—online coaching program

Easily discover your passion and purpose, overcoming barriers to success, and create a job or business you love with my self-paced online course.

Gain unlimited lifetime access to this course, for as long as you like—across any and all devices you own. Be supported by me and gain practical, inspirational, easy-to-access strategies to achieve your dreams.

To start achieving outstanding personal and professional results with absolute certainty and excitement. **Click here to enrol or find out more—the-coaching-lab.teachable.com/p/follow-your-passion-and-purpose-to-prosperity**

ALSO BY THE AUTHOR

Transformational Super Kids:

The Little Princess
The Little Princess Can Fly
I Have to Grow
The Boy Who Cried

Mid-Life Career Rescue:

The Call for Change
What Makes You Happy
Employ Yourself
Job Search Strategies That Work
3 Book Box Set: The Call for Change, What Makes You Happy, Employ Yourself
4 Book Box Set: The Call for Change, What Makes You Happy, Employ Yourself, Job Search Strategies That Work

Master Life Coach:

Leonardo da Vinci: Life Coach
  Coco Chanel: Life Coach

The Art of Living:
How to Find Your Joy and Purpose
How to Find Your Passion and Purpose
How to Find Your Passion and Purpose Companion Workbook
Career Rescue: The Art and Science of Reinventing Your Career and Life
Boost Your Self-Esteem and Confidence
Anxiety Rescue
No! Why 'No' is the New 'Yes'
How to Find Your Joy and Purpose
How to Find Your Joy and Purpose Companion Workbook

The Art of Success:

Leonardo da Vinci
Coco Chanel

Journaling Prompts Series:

The Passion Journal
The Passion-Driven Business Planning Journal
How to Find Your Passion and Purpose 2 Book-Bundle Box Set

Health & Happiness:

The Happy, Healthy Artist
Stress Less. Love Life More
Bounce: Overcoming Adversity, Building Resilience and Finding Joy
Bounce Companion Workbook

Mindful Sobriety:

Mind Your Drink: The Surprising Joy of Sobriety

Mind Over Mojitos: How Moderating Your Drinking Can Change Your Life:Easy Recipes for Happier Hours & a Joy-Filled Life

Happy Sobriety:
Happy Sobriety: Non-Alcoholic Guilt-Free Drinks You'll Love
The Sobriety Journal
Happy Sobriety Two Book Bundle-Box Set: Alcohol and Guilt-Free Drinks You'll Love & *The Sobriety Journal*

Money Manifestation:

Financial Rescue: The Total Money Makeover: Create Wealth, Reduce Debt & Gain Freedom

The Prosperous Author:

Developing a Millionaire Mindset
Productivity Hacks: Do Less & Make More
Two Book Bundle-Box Set (Books 1-2)

Miracle Mindset:

Change Your Mindset: Millionaire Mindset Makeover: The Power of Purpose, Passion, & Perseverance

Non-Fiction:
Where is Salvator Mundi?
More of Cassandra's practical and inspiring workbooks on a range of career and life enhancing topics can be found on her website (www.cassandragaisford.com) and her author page at all good online bookstores.

FURTHER RESOURCES

SURF THE NET

www.heartmath.org - comprehensive information and tools to help you access your intuitive insight and heart based knowledge. Validated and supported by science-based research.

www.whatthebleep.com – a powerful and inspiring site emphasising quantum physics and the transformational power of thought.

www.greggbraden.com – New York Time bestselling author Gregg Braden is a rare mix of scientist, visionary and scholar with the ability to speak to your mind, while touching the wisdom of your heart.

www.entrepreneur.com/howto—your go to place for all the latest tips and strategies from leading experts

www.gettingthingsdone.com—the official home of the work-life management system that has helped countless individuals and organisations bring order to chaos.

www.venusclubs.co.nz—a business community designed to help women in business thrive.

www.lifereimagined.org—loads of inspiration and practical tips to help you maximise your interests and expertise, personalised and interactive.

ACKNOWLEDGMENTS

This book (and my new life) was made possible by the amazing generosity, open heartedness and wonderful friendship of so many people. Thank you!

To all the amazingly, interesting clients who have allowed me to help them over the years. Your feedback, deep sharing, requests for help and inspired, courageous action, continues to inspire me.

Thank you also to my terrific friends and supporters, especially to my new writing friends. Without your help and cheerleading I would have struggled.

My special thanks to Claudia Svatefoss for your amazing encouragement and help. You really are positively perfect. Barry Watson, thank you for inviting me to become part of an inspiring group of authorpreneurs. Holly Hall, thank you for rescuing my cover. And Cate Walker – thank you again for volunteering your proofreading skills.

My daughter Hannah, I wish for you everything that your heart desires. Without you I doubt I would ever have accomplished all the things I have in my life.

And to the love of my life - Lorenzo, my Templar Knight. Thank you for believing in me.

Here's to an extra-ordinary level of happiness and contentment in all lives.

ABOUT THE AUTHOR

CASSANDRA GAISFORD is best known as *The Queen of Uplifting Inspiration.*

She is a holistic therapist, award-winning artist, and #1 bestselling author. A corporate escapee, she now lives and works from her idyllic lifestyle property overlooking the Bay of Islands in New Zealand.

Cassandra's unique blend of business experience and qualifications (BCA, Dip Psych.), creative skills, and wellness and holistic training (Dip Counselling, Reiki Master Teacher) blends pragmatism and commercial savvy with rare and unique insight and out-of-the-box-thinking for anyone wanting to achieve an extraordinary life.

Writing as Mollie Mathews (www.molliemathews.com), she is also known by her fans for her "sensual, beautiful, empowered stories enveloped in true romance." Her love stories have resonated with a global audience. She has been featured in magazines, television, and radio. A graduate of Victoria University, she has given keynote speeches at romance writers conventions and international seminars.

Mollie passionately believes in the power of romance to transform people's lives. Her stories are unashamedly positive, optimistic, full of fun and sizzling passion.

Both Cassandra and Mollie love all the arts, traveling, orchids, and all things inspiring, uplifting, and beautiful.

FREE WORKBOOK!

The Passion Journal: The Effortless Path to Manifesting Your Love, Life, and Career Goals

Thank you for your interest in my new book.
To show my appreciation, I'm excited to be giving you another book for FREE!

Download the free *Passion Journal Workbook* here>>https://dl. bookfunnel.com/aepj97k2n1

I hope you enjoy it—it's dedicated to helping you live and work with passion, resilience and joy.

You'll also be subscribed to my newsletter and receive free giveaways, insights into my writing life, new release advance alerts and inspirational tips to help you live and work with passion, joy, and prosperity. Opt out at anytime.

STAY IN TOUCH

Become a fan and Continue To Be Supported, Encouraged, and Inspired

Subscribe to my newsletter and follow me on BookBub (https://www.bookbub.com/profile/cassandra-gaisford) and be the first to know about my new releases and giveaways

www.cassandragaisford.com
www.facebook.com/cassandra.gaisford
www.instagram.com/cassandragaisford
www.youtube.com/cassandragaisfordnz
www.pinterest.com/cassandraNZ
www.linkedin.com/in/cassandragaisford
www.twitter.com/cassandraNZ

And please, do check out some of my videos where I share strategies and tips to stress less and love life more—http://www.youtube.com/cassandragaisfordnz

I invite you to share your stories and experiences in our Career

Rescue Community. We'd love to hear from you! To join, visit https://www.facebook.com/Career_Rescue

BLOG

Subscribe and be inspired by regular posts to help you increase your wellness, follow your bliss, slay self-doubt, and sustain healthy habits.

Learn more about how to achieve happiness and success at work and life by visiting my blog:

www.cassandragaisford.com/archives

SPEAKING EVENTS

Cassandra is available internationally for speaking events aimed at wellness strategies, motivation, inspiration and as a keynote speaker.

She has an enthusiastic, humorous and passionate style of delivery and is celebrated for her ability to motivate, inspire and enlighten.

For information navigate to www.cassandragaisford.com/contact/speaking

To ask Cassandra to come and speak at your workplace or conference, contact: cassandra@cassandragaisford.com

NEWSLETTERS

For inspiring tools and helpful tips subscribe to Cassandra's free newsletters here:
http://www.cassandragaisford.com

Sign up now and receive a free eBook to help you find your passion and purpose!
http://eepurl.com/bEArfT

PLEASE LEAVE A REVIEW

Word of mouth is the most powerful marketing force in the universe. If you found this book useful, I'd appreciate you rating this book and leaving a review.

Great reviews help people find good books.

Thank you so much! I appreciate you!

PS: If you enjoyed this book, could you do me a small favour to help spread the word about it and share on Facebook, Twitter and other social networks.

COPYRIGHT

Published by Blue Giraffe Publishing 2020

Blue Giraffe Publishing is a division of Worklife Solutions Ltd.

Cover Design by Cassandra Gaisford

Neither the publisher nor the author are engaged in rendering professional advice or services to the individual reader. The ideas, procedures, and suggestions contained in this book are not intended as a substitute for psychotherapy, counselling, or consulting with your physician.

The intent of the author is only to offer information of a general nature to help you in your quest for emotional, physical, and spiritual well-being.

Any use of information in this book is at the reader's discretion and risk. Neither the author nor the publisher can be held responsible for any loss, claim or damage arising out of the use, or misuse, of the suggestions made, the failure to take medical advice or for any material on third party websites.

ISBN PRINT: 978-0-9951072-8-1
   ISBN EBOOK: 978-0-9951072-7-4
   ISBN Hardcover: 978-0-9951250-0-1

First Edition